and Suddenly
the change

By: Chad Smith

Every word in this book was written by me. No AI was used for ideas or editing.
This comes from the heart.

To find more books by me visit:

www.gattaca.world

Copyright 2025

For Jovan Mrvos

&

Kat

Intro

This was me attempting to write some happy poetry.

My last two collections have been pretty dark.

It didn't work out.

This is a warning for you, as it should have been for me.

It gets dark out here, wandering on the boundaries.

"When man discovered the mirror, he began to lose his soul."

- Emile Durkheim

Table of Contents

Part One

DEFEAT AT ALL LANES
24
Dear P
I Knew
Shaking in a bed
Reefs
Instagram
Boundaries I Can't Know
Carefully carved out glass
Double Nickels
And all the Bad Things

Part Two

Chasing Lightning on the Run Back

It was nothing

With Every Storm

Finding Sky

and we drank

The Day After

Falling through the seams

the band across the street

Sterile

Part One

"As soon as one does not kill oneself, one must keep silent about life."

- Albert Camus

"The bird is gone, and in what meadow does it now sing?"

- Dick, Philip K. Flow My Tears, the Policeman Said. Houghton Mifflin Harcourt, 2012.

DEFEAT AT ALL LANES

I need milk
    someone once told
        me

that if I drank
    enough

it will offset
    the effects
        of all these pills

made in bath tubs
    blue
        stamped
            with car emblems

if I can keep
    it down

going into open lanes
    sometimes
        hard for me to navigate

it's hard to
    decide
        where to
            merge

where
    to go

especially these
    grey lanes
        gritty

            and snow covered.

24

In 24 thoughts
    you start to forge
        some sort of bond
            with the people
                across from you.

In 24 minutes
    you are going walk
        across the room
            and order another glass
                of Pinot Noir.

In 24 minutes
    you will finally decide
        whether or not
            to stay.

In 24 minutes
    you are going to
        step out onto
            the balcony.

And in 24 seconds
    you are going to
        look up into a sky
            stars blurred out by city lights
                peer off the edge
                and

                        decide.

Dear P

remember that time
we were doing
        mushrooms in July?

I was lying naked in the driveway
staring at stars

"You idiot" you said
and then joined me

we took turns
        singing
                old Pink Floyd songs

and trying to
        drown
                out
                      our lives.

still, the selfish prick that
        I am

I wish you were here

I need your advice

but I do know when
you come to see me
        if only for a moment.

I am now
        like you
damaged
        beyond
              repair.

But oh God
the moment I caught
        Debbie

in your driveway
all the despair
        we could muster
will always
        shake me

and how I
        wish you were still here.

I Knew

that day
    I had
        kept calling

and you didn't answer

I left work early
    and drove home
        in my demo car
            from the dealer

in a grey rain

I wondered
    if rain drops
        feel pain
            when they break
                onto windshields

up the stairs
    concrete

I opened
    our green apartment door

and you
    who I new
        the fragments
            and softness
                of touch

on the floor
    white oval pills

        everywhere

red vomit
    and your eyes blank

I saw the dark
    and
        fell
            to the floor

I still don't
    remember
        the next three days.

Shaking in a bed

when your body
loses the ability
to control itself
when you're awake
the terror and the flailing
exhausts me.

everyone tells me I'm
      not doing fine
everyone tells me I'm
      not the same anymore

I wake up at 3am
and walk through the dark house
sometimes with a golden retriever
but often alone

I am looking for me.

navigating this dark air
around red couches
and glass tables

I cannot
      find
            what I'm looking for.

Reefs

it was on that beach
with the sand
      so fine
almost silken
grains
from an Egyptian tomb
pink and white
sometimes
pointing at the sun
I washed up dead
my head
had hit a reef
bleached white
by warming seas
deep into my
white bone.

Instagram

I found you
trapped in the dirt
behind the black iron bars

the green grass
behind
you

you were naked
filthy with dirt

and I don't know
why you chose
these ice white cloud
walls

clear
so people
could
leer at you

and you

with no freedom

Boundaries I Can't Know

blurred streaks of red
    and blue
        and yellow

flash by me
    as the wipers
        try
to keep the windshield
    from giving up

rushing toward home
    the white hash marks
        blur to one

I took too many
    pills
dark
    and dreamy

a large truck
    in front of me
hums and seems
    to vanish
into the horizon

passing into a boundary
    I cannot know

the constant road hiss
    sprays from my leaders
as I spray my followers
    with heaven's tears

another turn
        onto another interstate

lonely
        no red lights in my head

no headlights
        in my rearview.

Carefully carved out glass

and sometimes
      it gets so cold here
on these cut glass
Estes Park winter mornings
that my toes go
      numb

on the grey wood floors

and other times
I remember
riding a horse through the back

wood fences
      breath just frost

we used to call them

Winter Defeats.

Double Nickels
(Title stolen from Jovan Mrvos)

I feel them coming
      soon

but for now it's
      the big one before
           ending in a zero.

now after all
      these post
           trauma mornings

I sit and argue
      with myself

sometimes I am a deer
      brown and white spotted
           steam through my nostrils

sometimes I am a black bear
      rubbing my back
           against a dark tree

sometimes I am a golden lab
      lying in a ditch
           shimmering with red.

And all the Bad Things
(Views from the back of an ambulance Take Two)

this trauma gurney
      with silver aluminum rails
and a curved yellow mattress

I am strapped down

the illness has made me skinny
      and I am easy to lift
into the truck

locked down with
      seatbelt-like straps

it's cold in here

to my left I see
      clear tubes and syringes

to my right I see
      plastic containers
          full of IV bags and drugs

just enough to keep
      the machine beeping
          behind me
to a sinus rhythm

until they can
        pass me off

through doors
        down a hallway.

Part Two

"Everything under heaven is in utter chaos; the situation is excellent."

- Mao Zedong

"When I saw your strand of hair I knew that grief is love turned into an eternal missing."

- Lupton, Rosamund. Sister. Crown Publishers, 2010.

Chasing Lightning on the Run Back

do you remember

racing back to the barn

with the red and black doors

and cloud blue rafters

our brown and white mares

trying to outrun

each other?

the wind picking up

cooling

racing the lighting

we called it

and sometimes we did

the sky indigo and violent

white cracks across the sky

It was nothing

looking up at

        these mirror buildings

in Manhattan

on Fifth

the bright evenings

our breath poof white

        in the winter air

so little I could ever

        capture of you

you were headed down paths

        I could not

                follow

our feet on the sidewalks

        and I feared

                as I moved

that you would never change

and was it my fault?

was I clinging?

was I paying attention?

coming to meet you

at that bright gold bar

    on the thirty-third floor

you and I snuggled

    against

        each other

easy smiles

and red wine

    leaning into each other

we couldn't get

    close enough

inhaling you

    sent paralysis

into

    all of me

"It was nothing"

    you always said.

but some nights

    I have these

        dreams.

With Every Storm

sometimes when

I think of houses

I think of a duplex

    red brick

with a stone wall

    in the back

        holding up

            dirt

in the back yard

and thick green oaks

    so close to the house

doors so heavy

    they were impossible

        to slam

no matter how hard

    my father tried

and all those trees

        sending leaves

splat

        splatt

                splattering

into the picture window

with every storm

I wonder if those walls

still contain

        all those

                screams.

Finding Sky

    these words

so often

    written

        out of order

like a second grader

    in a small desk

writing the best

    they have

words strung

    into

        meaningless

    patterns

drifting now

    that one night

        midnight blue

my little globe

split

      splittered

           splittering

on the floor

the cold water

      spilling

across

      my bare feet

sticky

    and

        sweet.

and we drank

fizz

    fuzz

        bizz

            buzz

this champagne

    pops bubbles into the air

poof

and long ago

on a California night

    we sat together

in your rented convertible

    and drove into the hills

listening to road music

you shaking your blonde mane

I popped a cork

    and you laughed

I poured two glasses

and we drank

slipping

    further up the coast

into the coastline of

    Half Moon Bay

        darkness.

The Day After

we found out

    I had been

night swimming

    off Vilano Beach

        in St. Augustine

only a partial moon

    but it was enough

and the waves roared

    but were only two feet

        off the back

I cut my heel

    on a shell

and it must have been

    around the time

        you died

the drugs

      had taken hold

and you fell

      bouncing

down that brown

      wooden

           flight of stairs.

in that house

      we threw

           so many parties in.

Falling through the seams

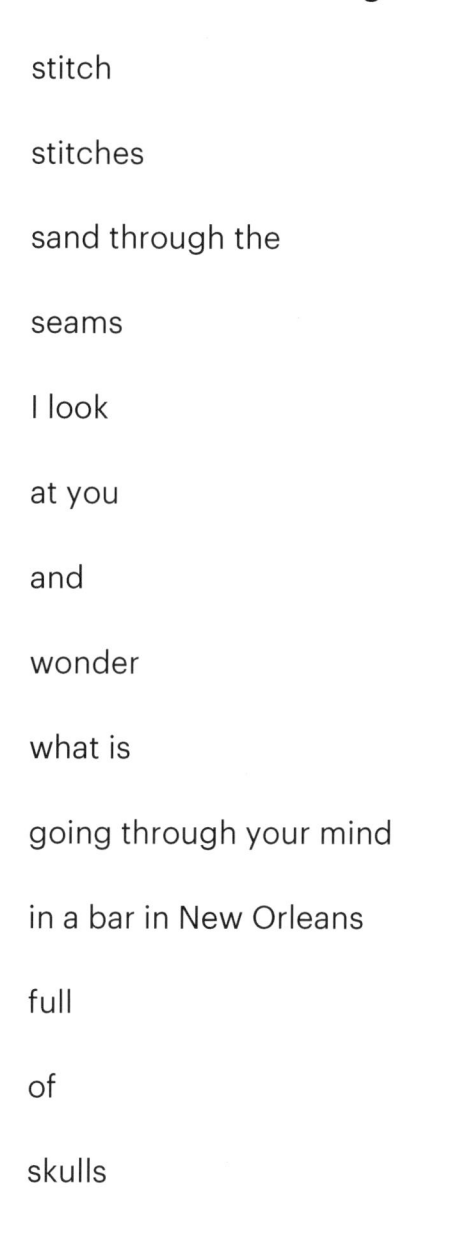

stitch

stitches

sand through the

seams

I look

at you

and

wonder

what is

going through your mind

in a bar in New Orleans

full

of

skulls

the band across the street

I step skit

skitt

    skittering

the tiny gravel

    on my feet

and I feel you

your hand ghosts

    into mine

and I remember

    your hair

and how you would

    flip it

across my shoulders

and the press

    of your skin at 3am

and you disappear

poof

the band keeps playing

and I just wish...

    I shiver

           cold

and bow my head.

Sterile

they don't tell you about those rooms

where you go to

identify

    a body

shaking

    eyes closed as you get close

        to the room

where the blue-green beds

    lie

        everywhere

and my sister

    covered

        with a sheet

eyes like cereal milk

    skin like shimmer

hair in clumps

    caked with something

        Red

just another day in the office

    for the man in blue scrubs

        behind

            me.

Epilogue

"And once the storm is over you won't remember you how made it through, how you managed to survive. You won't even be sure, in fact, whether the storm is really over. But one thing is certain. When you come out of the storm you won't be the same person who walked in. That's what the storm's all about."

- Murakami, Haruki. Kafka on the Shore. Translated by Philip Gabriel, Vintage International, 2005.

Acknowledgments

This collection would not have happened without the encouragement of my wife Amiee and my TIRELESS early readers and editors Anastasia Smith, Bryan Center and Andrew Virdin. I love all of you.

Cover photo by Chad Smith.

About the Author

Chad Smith is a consultant and author hiding out in the Caribbean. He is married and has two neurotic golden retrievers.

Made in the USA
Columbia, SC
17 February 2025